cl☘verleaf books™

Holidays and Special Days

Chelsea's Chinese New Year

Lisa Bullard

illustrated by **Katie Saunders**

M MILLBROOK PRESS·MINNEAPOLIS

For Ashley —L.B.

Millbrook Press
A division of Lerner Publishing Group, Inc.
241 First Avenue North
Minneapolis, MN 55401 USA

For reading levels and more information, look up this title at www.lernerbooks.com.

Main body text set in Slappy Inline 18/28.
Typeface provided by T26.

Library of Congress Cataloging-in-Publication Data

Bullard, Lisa.
    Chelsea's Chinese new year / by Lisa Bullard ; illustrated by Katie Saunders.
        p.   cm. — (Cloverleaf books™ Holidays and special days)
    Includes index.
    ISBN: 978-0-7613-5078-1 (lib. bdg. : alk. paper); ISBN: 978-0-7613-8839-5 (EB pdf)
    1. Chinese New Year—Juvenile literature. 2. China-Social life and customs—Juvenile literature.
  3. United States—Social life and customs—Juvenile literature. I. Saunders, Katie ill. II. TItle.
  GT4905.B86 2012
  394.261—dc23   2011021513

Manufactured in the United States of America
4-49064-10789-2/6/2020

TABLE OF CONTENTS

Chapter One

Getting Ready

Hi, I'm Chelsea! My family is getting ready for a big holiday. It's called **Chinese New Year.**

Dad says it is **China's** most important holiday. Some people celebrate it in the United States too. Like me!

We sure are busy right now. We're cleaning **last year's bad luck** out of our house.

China

People in China have celebrated Chinese New Year for thousands of years. In that country, people call it Spring Festival. Lunar New Year is another name for the holiday.

Then we're going to buy new red clothes. Dad says **red** is for **good luck**.

Chapter Two
A Late Night

We've worked hard to get ready. Now it's the night before Chinese New Year. Even kids get to stay up really late tonight.

The date for Chinese New Year changes every year. It's based on an old Chinese calendar. It always starts at a time of month when we cannot see the moon from Earth. The holiday always takes place in January or February.

Last year, I fell asleep too early. This year, I want to **stay awake** for all the **fun**.

We're at my grandparents' house for this big night.
There are uncles, aunts, and cousins everywhere.
We talk and play games.

All of this **laughing** helps me keep my **eyes** open.

Family is the most important part of Chinese New Year. Some families also honor the gods and their ancestors. Ancestors are family members from long ago. Some people show honor by praying. Some people put out offerings of food.

We have a **big feast**. There's fish and lots of other food. Then everybody makes **dumplings**. They're like little cooked pillows with yummy stuff inside.

Some families make sure to leave some fish for leftovers. They believe they will then have extra food in the new year.

I can't wait to eat them at midnight.

BOOM! Pop! Firecrackers snap.
Fireworks light the sky. It's midnight.

Chinese New Year is here, and I'm still awake!

People tell different stories about how Chinese New Year started. One story tells of a monster named Nian. Nian showed up at New Year's time. But people learned how to scare Nian away. The monster was afraid of loud noises and the color red.

I finally fall asleep. In the morning, Mom and Dad give me a **red envelope**. Money falls out when I open it up.

Chinese New Year really is a lucky time!

Children often receive many red envelopes during Chinese New Year. The envelopes come from grown-up relatives, family friends, or neighbors.

Chinese New Year doesn't stop after one day.
We keep celebrating! We wear our new clothes.

Chinese New Year used to be fifteen days long. Some people no longer celebrate that whole time. But many people still celebrate for several days.

We take presents to friends and family.

We try to be very good. This starts the year out right.

Chapter Four

Parade!

Chinese New Year ends with a big **parade**. My favorite part is the dragon. Dad says **dragons are lucky** too.

Many Chinese men moved to California in the mid-1800s. They brought the Chinese New Year celebration to California. In modern times, the city of San Francisco has a big Chinese New Year parade each year. The parade's dragon is over 200 feet (60 meters) long!

I guess **Chinese New Year** is finally over.
But I have enough **LUCK** to last until next year!

An Animal for Each Year

Each year of the Chinese calendar matches up with one of twelve animals. The animal and year matchups start over every twelve years. People often decorate for Chinese New Year with pictures of the New Year's animal.

Can you figure out where your birthday fits in the chart below? Look to see which animal matches the year you were born. Then draw a picture of your animal!

January 22, 2004–February 8, 2005	Monkey
February 9, 2005–January 28, 2006	Rooster
January 29, 2006–February 17, 2007	Dog
February 18, 2007–February 6, 2008	Pig
February 7, 2008–January 25, 2009	Rat
January 26, 2009–February 13, 2010	Ox
February 14, 2010–February 2, 2011	Tiger
February 3, 2011–January 22, 2012	Rabbit
January 23, 2012–February 9, 2013	Dragon
February 10, 2013–January 30, 2014	Snake
January 31, 2014–February 18, 2015	Horse
February 19, 2015–February 7, 2016	Sheep

GLOSSARY

ancestor: a family member from long ago

celebrate: do something to show how special or important a day is

dragon: a make-believe animal that looks like a giant reptile with wings

dumplings: a food made from cooked dough and filled with meat or vegetables

honor: to give praise or show respect

lunar: to do with the moon

offering: a gift, often to a god or a leader

several: more than two, but not many

BOOKS

Jango-Cohen, Judith. *Chinese New Year.* Minneapolis: Carolrhoda Books, 2005. This book has more information about the legends behind Chinese New Year and the different ways people prepare for it.

Lin, Grace. *Bringing in the New Year.* New York: Alfred A. Knopf, 2008. Read this story to find out how another family celebrates Chinese New Year.

McGee, Randel. *Paper Crafts for Chinese New Year.* Berkeley Heights, NJ : Enslow Publishers, 2008. This book shows readers how to make gift envelopes, dragon puppets, and Chinese lanterns out of paper.

WEBSITES

Chinese Horoscopes
http://kids.nationalgeographic.com/kids/stories/peopleplaces/chinese-horoscopes
Find out even more about the animals connected to the Chinese calendar with this website from *National Geographic Kids*.

My Favorite Day—Chinese New Year
http://learnenglishkids.britishcouncil.org/en/short-stories/my-favourite-day-chinese-new-year
This website from the British Council shows you a story about a girl who enjoys Chinese New Year. You can also put together a puzzle.

Sagwa: Countdown to the New Year
http://pbskids.org/sagwa/games/countdown/index.html
Play fun Chinese New Year games on this website from PBS Kids.